LIT
JOURNEY ᴜᴘ ᴿ

Dorothy McRae-McMahon is a
minister in the Uniting Church in
Australia. For ten years she was a
minister with the Pitt Street Uniting
Church in the centre of Sydney and
then for five years the National
Director for Mission for her church.
She was a member of the World
Council of Churches Worship
Committee for its Canberra
Assembly and Moderator of its
Worship Committee for the Harare
Assembly.

Also by the author:

Being Clergy, Staying Human
(Alban Institute, Washington, Australia, 1992)

Echoes of Our Journey: Liturgies of the People
(The Joint Board of Christian Education, Melbourne, 1993)

The Glory of Blood, Sweat and Tears:
Liturgies for Living and Dying
(The Joint Board of Christian Education, Melbourne, 1996)

Everyday Passions: A Conversation on Living
(ABC (Australian Broadcasting Corporation) Books,
Sydney, 1998)

LITURGIES FOR THE JOURNEY OF LIFE

Dorothy McRae-McMahon

Published in Great Britain in 2000 by
Society for Promoting Christian Knowledge
Holy Trinity Church
Marylebone Road
London NW1 4DU

British Library Cataloguing-in-Publication Data

A catalogue record for this book is available from
the British Library

ISBN 0–281–05277–8

Typeset by Pioneer Associates, Perthshire
Printed in Great Britain by
The Cromwell Press, Trowbridge

Contents

INTRODUCTION   ix

A SUNDAY AT PRAYER   1
Worship for Sunday morning   3
Liturgy for Holy Communion   8
Evening worship   13

WE ARE NOT ALONE   17
We are not alone   19
The feast of God   23
Celebrating the family   28
Celebrating creation   32
We are the ones who are loved   36
Mission: the holy ground of God   40
The reigning of love   44
Celebrating our community   48
The golden ones   51

HARD TIMES, SAD TIMES   57
Liturgy for hard journeys   59
Dare to feel the longings   63
A service of healing   66
Light a candle   70
An anointing   75
A simple funeral   78

THE CHRISTIAN YEAR   83
Liturgy for Advent   85
Liturgy for Christmas Day   91
Liturgy for Good Friday   95
Liturgy for Easter   101
Liturgy for Pentecost   105

ENDINGS – AND NEW BEGINNINGS   113
Being born again   115
And the dance goes on   119
In the end – there is a passion   122
Beginning a new journey together   126

Index of themes   *129*
Index of resources for worship   130

*For my forebears of the clan McRae – the
children of grace who, according to the stories,
produced many priests, poets and people
who defended to the death the things
in which they believed.*

Introduction

Perhaps it does not need to be said that part of the essential power of liturgical life is that it is corporate. Obviously, private times of worship and contemplation are important to many of us and have a different function in the formation and sustaining of our life. For some people this private interface between themselves and the source of renewal seems to be enough. However, most of us long to believe and to discover that we are not, in the end, alone. We need the corporate experience of worship or some other ritual of corporate life (even football or the pub!).

When people come together before their God and each other as an experience of community, we often find that the love and courage and truth which is released goes beyond the sum total of our human hopes. Effective liturgy enhances the possibility that this dynamic of engagement with God and each other may take place.

In rituals of healing and forgiveness there is also something of an enacting of faith. We, who find it hard to believe in our forgiveness, or healing, or some other hope, commit ourselves in faith to affirming before others that we are forgiven or healed or given a new hope. This corporate enacting of our faith can often bring into being the matter which is the focus of our faith. It is rather like a marriage. The witnesses to the marriage not only celebrate the faith that this relationship is possible, they affirm that they have seen this love, they support it into the future and they take part in the making significant of the moment of commitment. So it is with many rituals with which we mark the passages of our life, large and small. In the ritual, we give dignity to the human journey and name it as truly significant before our God.

ABOUT THESE LITURGIES

All the liturgies in this book have arisen in response to the life journeys of individuals, groups of people or congregations. Some of them come from the life of the people of the Pitt Street Uniting Church in the centre of Sydney in the time of my ministry with that church. Some have emerged from the life of the national staff of the Uniting Church during the period when I was its Director for Mission. Others have come from individuals and groups of people across the churches or in the wider community. Two were inspired by my time as a member of the Worship Committee of the Canberra Assembly of the World Council of Churches.

USING THESE LITURGIES

If symbols are explicitly used in these liturgies, they are listed at the beginning of each one. However, it is assumed that you will add your own ideas for cloths, candles, flowers – that you will make the environment for worship beautiful in your own ways.

Apart from rather well-known Taizé chants and similar music which is integral to some liturgies, music, songs and hymns are not included. Those that are included can be found in *In Spirit and in Truth*, World Council of Churches, 1991, and *Songs and Prayers from Taizé*, Mowbray, 1991. What Christians sing, even within one country and tradition, varies so much these days that it did not seem helpful to put my ideas there. You will best know where you usually sing and what singing is part of the spirituality of your congregation or group.

If these liturgies resonate with the life journeys around you, take them and make them your own. Add to them your own imagination and the symbols and the prayers which genuinely arise from the life where you are. Some liturgy becomes part of the great tradition of the Church. Some, like the liturgies in this book, are meant to be shaped and reshaped so that they breathe with the life of the people.

My thanks to Sue Parks of SPCK, John Bell of the Iona Community, Brian Wren the British hymn writer, and Terry Macarthur of the WCC for their encouragement in believing that my liturgies could be useful to others and that this book could be.

Dorothy McRae-McMahon

A Sunday at Prayer

Here God dwells among the people.
God will make a home among us
and we shall be God's people.
God is the beginning and the end
and is making the whole creation new.
Let us worship together!

WORSHIP FOR SUNDAY MORNING

CALL TO WORSHIP

Do you see this city?
Here God dwells among the people.
**God will make a home among us
and we shall be God's people.**

God is the beginning and the end
and is making the whole creation new.
Let us worship together!

CONFESSION

In penitence and faith we come before you, Holy God, and say:
'This is who we are.'
We are the people
who long for the new heaven and the new earth
but can't always take the first step towards it.
Forgive us, gracious God.

We are those who love the city
but who participate in its destructive patterns of life
and fail to lift up its beauty and creativity.
Forgive us, gracious God.

We are the people who commit ourselves
to build the community of the Gospel
but we so often betray that hope
and fail each other.
Forgive us, gracious God.

We are those who sometimes see the vision
for our own lives
but we are weak and fall far short
of the dream.
Forgive us, gracious God.

ASSURANCE OF PARDON

In Jesus Christ, we may always announce
that now is the time of the new heaven
and the new earth.
The old order has passed away
and the new creation is before us.
Thanks be to God!

THE LORD'S PRAYER

READINGS

Old Testament
Epistle

SENDING OUT OF THE CHILDREN

The children gather at the front

We send you out to learn
that God loves the world
and all its people
and that God loves you.
Amen.

GOSPEL

SERMON

AFFIRMATION OF FAITH

In response to the word, let us stand and affirm our faith:

All:

**In desert and forest, mountain and water,
we see the signs that God is with us.
In grass that grows through cities of concrete,
we see the signs that God is with us.
In the faces of people whom God so loves,
we see the signs that God is with us.
In our brokenness,
there is the hope of wholeness.
In our emptiness,
there is the hope of fullness.
In our deaths,
lies the hope of resurrection life.
This is the Word in Christ to us.
The flame of the Holy Spirit
lives in this place
and travels with us.
Amen.**

PRAYERS OF INTERCESSION

Let us pray.
O God, who looked upon the city of Jerusalem
and wept over it,
stand with us as we look at our city
and our world.
For we long to see a new heaven and a new earth.

We see the pain and struggle of the people
bowed down by exploitation and conflict.
We hear the groaning of the creation
as it waits for new life and hope.
Make us part of your new creation, O God.

We see the city and hear its sounds around us.

Silence

We picture its skyline and landscape in all its beauty
and feel that pulse of its life
moving and stopping,
despairing and hoping,
laughing and crying,
with all its possibilities for community
and all its possibilities for alienation.
We love our city, gracious God.
Be with us at its heart
and reveal to us the signs of your presence.

We see your Church,
in all its humanness,
standing in divided witness still,
struggling to understand
the gospel for this day and this place.
Recreate us, O God,
and send to us your liberating Spirit.

Each one of us, in our own place, O God,
sees the need and hears the cry of humanity.
Let those who will
lift up their prayers for the Church
and the world . . .

People offer their prayers

We see ourselves, O God,
people of faith and faithlessness
dancing in the sun one day
and overwhelmed by our realities on the next,
joyfully announcing the gospel sometimes
and then trembling in our uncertainty.
We see the hope that lies among us
the hope that we could care
and live in community with each other
and the world.

Give life to this hope in us, God of community.
Bring to us a celebration of all that is,
in its ambiguity, its frailty and its costliness.
Amen.

OFFERING

Let us offer our gifts as a sign
of our commitment to Christ
and the world.

PRAYER OF DEDICATION

All standing

Let us praise God.
O God, who calls us from death to life,
we give ourselves to you
and with the Church through all ages,
we thank you for your saving love
in Jesus Christ.
Amen.

BLESSING AND DISMISSAL

The night shall be no more
and we will need no light from lamps.
For God is our light,
and always walks before us.

Go forth into the light
and share in the recreating of the world.
And may God the beginning give you a new day,
God the Christ take you by the hand
and God the Spirit give you energy and peace.
Amen.
Amen.

LITURGY FOR HOLY COMMUNION

GREETING

The peace of Christ be with you.
And also with you.

CALL TO WORSHIP

All standing

We are always a broken body,
but we are the body of Christ.

With the faithful who go before us,
we are the body of Christ.

In Christ is our unity.
In Christ is our wholeness.
Thanks be to God!

CONFESSION

As we come before God in confession,
let us reflect on the symbols at the centre of our life.

The bread and wine are brought to the table

Silence

In our failure to be the Church of love and grace,
**we drink a common cup
and break the common loaf.**

In our sharing in injustice and violence
against the people of the world,
**we drink a common cup
and break the common loaf.**

In our lack of faith and courage
to follow the way of the cross,
**we drink a common cup
and break the common loaf.**

ASSURANCE OF PARDON

In our brokenness
and in our humanness,
the Christ is one with us.
In Christ we are set free.
In Christ we are enough to be the Church.
Amen.

GLORIA

READINGS

Old Testament
Epistle

SENDING OUT OF THE CHILDREN

The children gather at the front

We send you out together
as our loved children
to learn, to play,
and as part
of the family of God.
Amen.

GOSPEL

SERMON

AFFIRMATION OF FAITH

In response to the word, let us stand and affirm our faith.

All:

The people of God have a human face.
We laugh,
we weep,
we wait in hope.
We lift our eyes,

and stub our toes,
we love,
and struggle,
we fail,
we stand
and always we stand
on trembling ground.

But God is God
and Jesus is the Christ
and the Spirit
will lift up our feet.
God is in the centre,
God is at our endings.
Nothing lies beyond
the love of God in Christ.

PRAYERS OF INTERCESSION

Let us bring before God
our prayers of intercession.

Come, Holy Spirit, renew the whole creation.
Send the wind and flame
of your transforming life
to lift up the Church in this day.
Give wisdom and faith
that we may know
the great hope to which we are called.
Come, Holy Spirit,
renew the whole creation.

Spirit of love, set us free
to emerge as the children of God.
Open our ears
that we may hear the weeping
of your creation.
Open our mouths
that we may be a voice
for the voiceless.

Open our eyes
that we may see your vision
of peace and justice.
Make us alive with the courage and faith
of your prophetic truth.
Come, Holy Spirit,
renew the whole creation.

Spirit of unity,
reconcile your people.
Give us the wisdom
to hold to what we need
to be your Church.
Give us the grace
to lay down
those things that we
can do without.
Give us a vision of your breadth
and length and height
which will challenge our smallness of heart
and bring us humbly together.
Come, Holy Spirit,
renew the whole creation.

Spirit of truth,
lift up your light among us.
May we ever be
a true reflection of the gospel
and lead the Church
into honest encounter with itself
and the world it claims to serve.
Come, Holy Spirit,
renew the whole creation.
Amen.

OFFERTORY
Let us bring our offerings to God.

The offering is received

BLESSING

May the Holy God surprise you on the way,
Christ Jesus take you by the hand,
and the Spirit lift up your life.
Amen.
Amen.

EVENING WORSHIP

GREETING

The peace of God be with you all.
And also with you.

OPENING SENTENCES

The transforming winds of creative life
are but the breath of God.

The passionate flames of justice and love
are the graceful signs of the Christ.

The flights of freedom in movements of truth
are the joyful life of the Spirit.

All:

We celebrate this day
and the signs of God in our midst.

CONFESSION

Let us remember who we are
before the holiness of God.

'Santo, Santo, Santo', *sung twice: once in Spanish, once in English
(WCC); or a similar chant from Taizé*

Silent reflection

Let us pray.
Holy God,
we have failed to live in full
the generosity of your grace,
the costliness of your love
and the liberation of your free spirit.
Forgive us, and lead us into life.
Amen.

ASSURANCE OF PARDON

Nothing can separate us
from the love of God in Christ Jesus.
In faith,
lay down the burden of this day
and enter the night in peace.
Amen.
Amen.

READINGS

REFLECTION

PRAYERS OF INTERCESSION

Come, Holy Spirit, in your renewing power.
Move in our labouring
with the energy of your being
and bring to birth in us
the true life of your Church.
Come, Holy Spirit,
in your renewing power.

Move in the world
with the streams of your justice.
Give waters of life to the poor
and rivers of freedom to the oppressed.
Come, Holy Spirit,
in your renewing power.

Move in our hearts
with the fire of your love.
Spread the warmth of your healing
and the flame of your transforming life.
Come, Holy Spirit,
in your renewing power.
In the name of Christ.
Amen.

LITANY FOR THE NIGHT

The night is the cover of your peace, O God,
the rhythm of your rest for all your people.

The darkness is the cloak of your gentleness, O God,
the warmth of your hand around the earth.

In its blackness, is the sign of your eternity,
the never-ending living of your love.

In faith we go to sleep and leave our life to you.
In child-like trust we end our efforts of this day.
In our sleeping, be our company.
In our waking, be the gift of our new day.
Go in peace and may God go with you.
Christ Jesus take you by the hand,
and the Spirit be a cloud of grace around you.
Amen.

We Are Not Alone

We are the people who heal each other,
who grow strong together,
who name the truth,
who know what it means
to live in community,
moving towards a common dream
for a new heaven and a new earth
in the power of the love of God,
the company of Jesus Christ
and the leading of the Holy Spirit.

WE ARE NOT ALONE

This service is prepared to encourage people who are involved in the struggle for justice, peace and truth.

For this service you need

- *Three candles – white, purple and green.*
- *A symbol of common humanness to be shared – e.g. bread, water, earth.*

Note

If some of the responses of the people are too long for your group to say together, e.g. the Affirmation, have the leader say the main text and the people respond with 'We are not alone'.

OPENING SENTENCES

Let us remember who we are:

We are the people of dignity.
Down the ages we have been the people of God,
the people who know themselves to be called
to freedom, courage and truth.
**We light a white candle for that dignity
and the power of God in us.**

We are the people who weep
for the suffering of the world.
We are the people who walk with the Christ
towards all who grieve,
who are oppressed and exploited.

We light a purple candle
for those who suffer with the people
and the power of Christ is in us.

We are the people of hope and faith.
In the Spirit we celebrate our energy
and strength, our power to heal
and our calling to work with God
in the recreating of the world.
We light a green candle
for our hope in the Spirit.
We are not alone.

NAMING OUR WEEPING

Where is the pain in our lives?

The people name their fears, angers, areas of pain

You are not alone.
Your tears are our tears.

AFFIRMING OUR HOPE

Who are the people who have given us strength and courage,
who have created models?

The people name the people

These people walk with us.
We have company on the journey.

READING

AFFIRMATION OF FAITH

Let us affirm our faith in God:

We believe in God
who created and is creating the earth,
who so loved the world that Christ was sent
to live life with us
and the Spirit to be our strength.

God has favoured us and appointed us
to be a light to the peoples
and a beacon for the nations;
to open eyes that are blind,
and release captives from the prisons,
out of the dungeons where they live in darkness.

In solidarity with the people of God
around the world,
and in company with the other churches
in this city,
we name ourselves as those who, in Jesus Christ,
are enough to do the task
in this time and this place.

We have heard the call of Christ
to follow in the way of the cross.
In faith we lay down our fear,
our weakness and our lack of worth
and announce again
with those who have gone before us that,
'Where the Spirit of the Lord is, there is liberty.'

INTERCESSION

Let us ask God for help along the way:

Response, sung: 'Jesus, remember us' *(Taizé)*

COMMITMENT TO EACH OTHER

A symbol of common humanness is shared

In the face of all our realities:

**We are the people who heal each other,
who grow strong together,
who name the truth,
who know what it means
to live in community,
moving towards a common dream
for a new heaven and a new earth
in the power of the love of God,
the company of Jesus Christ
and the leading of the Holy Spirit.**

BLESSING

Go in peace,
as those who tread a common way with the Christ;
and may each stone on the road be firm under your feet
as God who is our rock,
the winds of the earth wrap you round with the breath of
the Spirit.
Amen.
Amen.

THE FEAST OF GOD
Agape meal

The people gather for the meal and the service is spread through the time of the meal while the people are seated at tables. People are encouraged to enjoy the meal by eating and talking together in the normal way. It is good to arrange for some people to be prepared to share stories of the life of the group or congregation, but to encourage spontaneous stories as well.

Needed for this service

- *One larger candle at each table, one lit small candle with a taper alongside, and a number of smaller 'tea' candles for lighting by those at the table. It is a good idea to have these gathered in the centre on a plate or tray.*
- *A large jug of water on each table and enough small glasses for each person. The jugs may need to be refilled during the meal.*

GREETING

The peace of Christ be with you.
And also with you.

OPENING SENTENCES

We are the people of the feast of God.
**The feast which feeds the hungry,
body, mind, heart and soul.
The feast which pours the water of life
into the thirsty depths of our being.**

We are those who are offered life in all its fullness.
Life to be shared in justice, freedom and peace.

In thanksgiving we gather.
The feast is for all.

The meal begins

After a period the leader invites the people to 'gather' others into the feast as follows

THE GATHERING IS NOT FINISHED

The gathering of God is for all who will come.
The celebration is for a hope
that is already won in Jesus Christ.
But we are not all here.
The hope of Jesus Christ is not yet complete in us.
Who do we long to gather into our community?

The people name people and groups who they long to invite into the feast of God

After each naming, a small candle is lit at the table where each speaker is seated

Gather all these we have named into our midst, O God.
Place them in our hearts and prayers,
place them in our working and struggling
to bring the whole world under your reign of love.
In faith, and in your name, O God,
we gather these, our sisters and brothers, into our feast.
Amen.

ASSURANCE OF PARDON

In Jesus Christ, even as we live in our brokenness,
we are called to be the guests at the table,
freed from the things that separate us
from each other and from God.
Come, eat, drink.
In faith, we are restored to the household of God.
Thanks be to God!

The meal goes on for a period

READINGS

Stories of celebration, or moments of achievement and hope are shared and people are invited to 'toast' each story as it is told

After the stories are concluded:

The living Word is among us,
even among us, who are ordinary human people.
The light of Christ is in our midst.
Thanks be to God!

A larger candle is lit on each table

AFFIRMATION OF FAITH

In response to the word, let us stand and affirm our faith:

We are made in the image of God,
echoes of the creator,
children of a loving energy,
one with the universe and all that lies within it.

Christ has been born in our earthiness,
seen in the face of justice,
vivid in our moments of truth,
dying and living in the passion of our life.

We can feel the power of the Spirit,
surrounding us with grace.
She is wise in the centre of our wanderings,
and joyfully gathering the whole creation
into the freedom of God.

This we believe.
This we affirm.
From this we will live.

The meal proceeds until shortly before the end

WE ARE TOGETHER

We are not alone.
We share the task and we share the nurturing gifts of God.
We share the common humanness
and we share the common hope in Christ.

Let us stand.
As we leave this place let us offer to each other
a glass of water from the jug in the centre of each table.
In this water lie the tears we share along the way.
They will be transformed into the water of life for us all.

Each person gives a glass of water to the person on their left with the words: **May this be the water of life for you.**

Let us pray:

Come close to where we stand, Jesus Christ.
Bring the hem of your robe against our fingers
that we may be healed, restored,
and filled with the energy and courage of your life.
Come close to us, Jesus Christ,
hope of the world.

Lay your hands on the world, O God.
Anoint it with your costly love.
If it is poor:
Flood it with your generous gifts.

If it is oppressed:
Break its chains of bondage,
turn them into barriers
to keep the people safe.

If it grieves:
Show it the face of your weeping
and the comfort of your Spirit.

Go with us into the world, O God,
that we may be your people,
as you are our God.
Amen.

COMMISSIONING AND BLESSING
Go in peace to love and serve the Christ and the world.

And may God the creator go on creating within us,
God in Jesus Christ, sit at table in our midst
and the Spirit lead us in the dance of life.
Amen.

The people pass the peace with each other as they go

CELEBRATING THE FAMILY

Needed for this service

- *A large candle.*

GREETING

We are all part of the rhythm of life:
we are born,
we give birth,
we live in relationships,
we search for meaning,
we make choices,
we die,
we suffer the loss of those we love.
As we celebrate this day of the journey,
peace be with you.
And also with you.

CALL TO WORSHIP

In your image we are made, creator God:
**male and female, young and old,
we are your creation.**

You took on our life, Jesus Christ.
**We find you there
in truth and grace within ourselves.**

You lead us on, Holy Spirit,
**in golden threads of life
in pain and joy.
Thanks be to God!**

CONFESSION

We had a dream about families, O God.
It looked like many lights
from a great stream of people,

generation after generation,
adding to each other's light,
warming each other's life,
setting each other free
across the boundaries
of all our differences,
creating in between
the brave and gracious light
of human community.

The candle is lit

Silent reflection

We are remembering how far we are from that dream.

Silent reflection

O God, so often it is the small
things that defeat us:
the lid off the toothpaste,
the bathmat in a heap,
one more unwiped bench,
the last grizzle from somebody,
another gift taken for granted.
These small things build upon each other, God,
and when our energy is low
and our hurts are high,
they take from our life.
It is often hard to live as families.
Lord, have mercy.
Lord, have mercy.

ASSURANCE OF PARDON

Hear the word of grace in Jesus Christ:
the love of God for us never fails.
Nothing can separate us from that love.
A new dream is always ours.
Rise up and live in freedom and faith.
Amen.

GLORIA

READINGS

SENDING OUT OF THE CHILDREN

The children gather at the front

We send you out to learn
that God loves the world
and all its people,
and that God loves you.
Amen.

SERMON

AFFIRMATION OF FAITH

In response to the word, let us stand and affirm our faith:

Birth comes through membranes of pain.
In the fragile claiming of life,
the drawing in of breath,
we are with God,
creator of heaven and earth,
maker of all that is.

Life comes through walking on,
and in the entering of death,
the daring to face our truths,
we are with Christ,
who died and lived with us,
who defeated death.

And in each moment of the way,
in lifting heart and freedom won,
in dreams untold and hopes of love,
the Spirit calls us on
with songs of life
and glimpses of community.

**We are the Church,
a family of faith.
Within this frail body,
we live in peace.**

PRAYERS OF INTERCESSION

In our homes, we are family,
in the Church, we are family,
in the community, we are family,
in the whole creation, we are family.
In every place, we depend on you, O God.
In faith we pray for the moments
in our life when we need your help.

The people offer their prayers

Response after each petition: **We pray for this
moment in our life**.

All these prayers,
and the silent prayers within our hearts,
we offer to you, O God of grace.
Show us the liberating love
which you give to us
that we may free each other
for life
and trustingly place in your hands
those who leave us in death.
O God, hear our prayer.

Sung: 'O Lord, hear our prayer' *(Taizé)*

SERVICE OF THE EUCHARIST

BLESSING

God go with you into this day,
Christ Jesus walk before you,
and the Spirit be a cloud of grace.
Amen.

CELEBRATING CREATION

For this service the church is decorated with things which celebrate the creation around where its people live and with other images and symbols of the creation in general. The children can be involved in this preparation and/or carry in and place things during the procession.

GREETING

The whole universe is a gift of God.
Everything here is a gift of God.
We are the gifts of God to each other.
We are all part of the procession of life.
Let us stand and celebrate by joining together
in the procession around the aisles of the church
as we sing the processional hymn.

CALL TO WORSHIP

Out of nothingness we came
through birth into life:
With the Spirit of God within us.

From the life of God
the universe unfolded into being:
With the Spirit of God within it.

From the heart of God
creation goes on till the end of time:
**With the Spirit of God within it
and with our spirit within it.**

Let us embrace the God who enfolds us.
We delight in God.

CONFESSION

Let us bring to God our confession:

Creator God,
we confess that our creating often goes wrong.

We are sometimes ignorant.
We are sometimes careless.
We are sometimes short-sighted
and self-interested.
Let us be aware of our failures in creation.

Silence

Let us name those things before God.

The people contribute

Forgive us, gracious God.
**We long to live in harmony
with all that you have given to us.**

ASSURANCE OF PARDON

God is always the creator
and the recreator.
**Let us celebrate the recreation
which is offered to us at this moment!**

READINGS WHICH CELEBRATE THE CREATION

STORIES AND IMAGES OF THE WONDERS OF CREATION
brought by several people, including children

SERMON

LITANY OF CREATION AND CREATING

Let us stand and affirm the wonder of creation together:

**God spoke light into the void
and the light is in our hands
against the darkness.
God clothed the world with sky
and we ride upon the wind
and breathe among the leaves.
God gifted us with earth**

and with water in between.
We dig and float
and drink and grow
and know the power of earth and sea.
We paint and sing and work and dance
in company with God.
We share the earth with all that is
in harmonies of warm and cold,
in green and desert,
crowd and lone,
we feel the pain,
we feel the joy.
God is our mother,
God is our father,
Christ is our brother,
the Spirit is within us.
We celebrate our sharing
in the recreating of the world.

PRAYERS OF INTERCESSION

Let us sit still among the pain of the world.

Silence

Let us name it.

Contributions from people

Beside each other, within the earth,
we are in her and of her,
are vulnerable with her,
are her people.
We are the people of pain and fear,
we are the people of anger and joy,
we are the people of compassion and grace.
We are each of us this,
we are all of us this,
we name our God,
we are one.

In all of us is a longing
for a life that has not yet come,
for a world that is free and just,
a dream of hope for all people.
Together with God
we will create that possibility.
Amen.

OFFERING

Let us give as those who receive.

The offering is received

DEDICATION

Receive these our gifts, gracious God.
In hope and thanksgiving
we offer them to you.
Amen.

BLESSING AND DISMISSAL

Go forth and share in
the recreating of the world.
We go in faith
to be the people of the new creation.

May the sun warm your soul
and the moon be gentle above you.
May the Creator hold your hand
and the Christ walk in your footsteps.
May the Spirit dance in your playing
and grace be found in your way.
Amen.
Amen.

WE ARE THE ONES WHO ARE LOVED
A celebration of our freedom to play

Needed for this service

Placed on the table:

- *Some small candles.*
- *A basket of gifts like flowers, fruits, sweets, balloons.*

GREETING

Christ be with you.
And also with you.

CALL TO WORSHIP

God who gave us the creation to play in,
with rolling landscapes of delight,
with wonders of earth and sea
and endless discoveries of beauty:
We worship you.

God who made us in infinite diversity,
with all the vivid colours of our differences,
all the magic of our unknowns
to be explored and celebrated:
We worship you.

God who in your being
carries the One who loved to feast with friends,
who sat in silence on the mountain tops alone,
whose Spirit dances in all the earth:
We worship you
in Spirit and in truth.

CONFESSION

O God, if we have taken your gifts for granted
and exploited them or used more than our due:
Forgive us.

If we have chosen to live driven lives,
refusing to stop and receive your peace and rest,
rushing past the delights you planned for our healing:
Forgive us.

Silent reflection

If we have failed to receive with hospitality
the strangers among us
who are never strange to you:
Forgive us and open our hearts to your grace.

ASSURANCE OF PARDON

The grace of God is infinite and free.
Rise up and live with faith and hope.
From the Spirit have we all received, grace upon grace.

THE WORD

Suggested readings: Psalm 65; Luke 15.11–32

AFFIRMATION OF FAITH

In response to the word, let us affirm our faith:

Life is a litany of love,
ringing in the moment of our birth,
sounding clear in the centre of our labouring,
calling us to bring forward the breaths of our beginning.
And we are the ones who are loved.
Thanks be to God.

The rhythm of love ripples on,
transforming our innocence into wisdom,
gasping into life again
as we survive the waves of harsh moments.

And we are the ones who are loved.
Thanks be to God.

We are the ones who are loved,
surrounded by countless gracious signs,
cherished in the gentle hands of God,
called again and again into joy.
This we believe,
from this we will live.
Thanks be to you Jesus Christ.

INTERCESSION

Let us pray for our ministry,
lighting a small candle for each place:

The people light the candles and name the place

Into your hands we give these ministries, O God:
inspire them with your Holy Spirit.
Take our gifts
and turn them into baskets of overflowing grace.

The basket of gifts is lifted up

Teach us to play, to rest, to be the people of the feast,
that we may be the ones of abundant life:
filled to overflowing with the generosity of your life,
living with lightness of being,
delighting in the colour, music, dancing and passion of
the creation.
Amen.

The gifts from the basket are shared around

BLESSING AND SENDING OUT

Go in faith, for there is God,
riding in the light on the water,
singing in the songs of the birds,
sitting in the midst of the parties of life.

We go in faith
to live in joyous freedom,
to play in the creation
and to drink deeply of the gracious cup of life.
Amen.

MISSION: THE HOLY GROUND OF GOD

GREETING

The peace of Christ be with you.
And also with you.

OPENING SENTENCES

The field of mission:
is the holy ground of God.

We tread this way with awe:
in the mystery of grace.

For walk we must, even in the silences:
following the call of the Christ.

CONFESSION

Voice 1:

We hear your voice, O Christ,
saying 'Whom will I send?'
and there is a longing in our hearts
to say 'Send us.'
But we have made so many mistakes
in our ignorance,
in our arrogance,
in our dividedness,
even in our enthusiasm
and we wonder whether
we should stand in silence on this,
your holy ground.

Silent reflection

Voice 2:

We have been saying so many things
for so many years, without much changing

and we wonder whether we should stand
in silence, on this, your holy ground
and stop our speaking,
and our writing
and our meetings.

Silent reflection

Voice 3:

We have been working so hard,
for so long
with small energies and few resources
and, when others rush past us without speaking
as though they will carry the gospel
beyond us and without us,
we wonder whether we should stand
in silence, on this, your holy ground
and close our circle behind them.

Silent reflection

Jesus remember us and forgive us.

Sung twice: 'Jesus, remember us' (Taizé)

ASSURANCE OF PARDON

Hear the word of God for us:
'I, the Lord, have called you in righteousness
and will hold your hand.
I will keep you
and give you as a covenant to the people.
Behold, the former things have come to pass
and new things I declare.
Before they spring forth,
I announce them to you.'
Thanks be to God!

Sung: 'Santo, Santo, Santo' (WCC)

READINGS

REFLECTION ON THE WORD

AFFIRMATION OF FAITH

In response to the word, let us stand
and affirm our faith:

We believe in light beyond our seeing,
flowing forth from the flame of life in God
who goes on creating in us
down through the ages of ages.

We believe in healing beyond our knowing,
from the Christ
whose robe stands close
to the reach of our hand
and the pain of our struggle
beyond the end of time.

We believe in the energy of God's Spirit,
stirring in our being
with a rhythm of courage and passion,
moving our feet
to risk Christ's way again
as those who are always called to be
the humble, human witnesses
to the faithfulness of God.

INTERCESSION

Mission belongs to you, O God.
The ground is holy
because you are already there.
All we are and all we do in faith
is dependent on you
and the victory already won.
We place ourselves in your hands again
and ask for all that we need to do the task.

The people name the gifts they need

We gather in our midst
those who are our partners in the task
and place them in your hands, loving God.

The people name their friends

Into our emptiness:
breathe your fullness.

Into our tiredness:
pour your energy.

If we are discouraged:
bring us your hope.

If we are afraid:
bring us your courage.

If we do not know the way:
give to us your wisdom.
For we are your people
and you are our God,
forever and forever.
Amen.

And now we pray your prayer as one:
Our Father . . .

BLESSING

Go into this day,
with a lifting of the heart.
And may the Triune God
be in our beginnings,
and endings,
and on the journey in between.
Amen.

THE REIGNING OF LOVE

This service is a Eucharist but can be adapted as a service of encouragement with a sharing of gifts, food, flowers of celebration.

GREETING

Christ be with you.
And also with you.

CALL TO WORSHIP

Now is the time of the feast!
**Call in all the people –
the oppressed, the hungry, the tired –
all who need our company
and the solidarity of God.**

Our God is generous.
The cup is full to overflowing,
the bread can be shared with all
and the dance of life comes after.
**Thanks be to God!
Let us worship in spirit and in truth.**

CONFESSION

Your presence, O God,
invites us to know more truly who we are.

A period of silence while we are open to that knowing

The world still waits in hunger and thirst, O God.
**Forgive our weakness.
Forgive our lack of faith.**

ASSURANCE OF PARDON

We worship a God of grace.
The word to us in Jesus Christ is –

Our sin is forgiven!
We celebrate our freedom!
We honour the holiness of God.

Sung 'Hosanna' or 'Alleluia'

READINGS

Old Testament
New Testament

GOSPEL

WITNESSES

Testimonies of the people – stories of the reigning of love

AFFIRMATION OF FAITH

In response to the word, let us stand and affirm our faith.
We believe that horizons of hope are never fixed.
They always move beyond,
in the creativity of God.

We believe that powers of evil cannot kill God.
God walks on free and leaps off our crosses
in the risen Jesus Christ.

We believe that the Spirit can never be confined.
She dances forth in the world
and is found in surprising places,
leading us on until the end of time.

PRAYERS OF INTERCESSION

Let us pray:

Come claim your ground, O holy God,
and show us more clearly your standing places.
We long to be one with you there.

Where are you among the homeless?
Where are you among the lost?
We long to be one with you there.

Where are you among the races?
Where are you among the cultures?
We long to be one with you there.

Where are you among the churches?
Where are you among the workers?
We long to be one with you there.

On the holy ground of the city
Come claim your people, O God.
**We offer ourselves as those who
try to walk with you.
Come create holy ground under our feet.
Amen.**

OFFERTORY

The bread, wine and gifts are brought to the table

The work of human hands is respected of God:
the bread, risen in the warmth,
the wine, crushed in its bitter sweetness.
All that we offer is received and transformed
into new possibilities.
Blessed be God forever!

GREAT THANKSGIVING

Christ be with you!
And also with you.

Lift up your hearts!
We lift them to our God.

Let us give thanks to the Holy God.
It is right to give our thanks and praise.

We give thanks to you, O God,
for your love for the world.
You look upon us all and name us good.
**You conceive in us a thousand possibilities
and carry us on into the timeless struggle
in bringing to birth the reigning of love.**

We thank you for Jesus Christ who gave hope
to ordinary people like us
and crashed through the boundaries
which separated us from life.
**With those who have gone before us
and those who will come after us,
we join the whole creation in the eternal hymn:**

'Holy, Holy, Holy' sung twice

THE EUCHARIST CONTINUES . . .

FINAL THANKSGIVING

Let us give thanks:

**We thank you, God, that you
never leave us hungry and thirsty.
We commit ourselves to so living in love
that all are fed and know your gracious community.
Amen.**

BLESSING

Go in peace in the power of Christ.
And may food be found beside the road,
living water rise forth in springs around you
and the Spirit restore you in the hard places.
Amen.

CELEBRATING OUR COMMUNITY

This service needs

- *A container of coals and incense (can be an earthenware dish placed on a heat resistant mat).*
- *A basket of small varied stones.*

OPENING SENTENCES

Let us gather our community around us –
The God of many names:

The people give their names for God

Those who have gone before us:

The people name their own 'saints' and mentors

Those who are with us in the places where we work:

The people name their colleagues

We are surrounded by a cloud of witnesses.
Their love enfolds us with light and fragrance.

The coals and incense are lit

We are living stones in the building of the holy city of God.

The basket of stones is placed in the centre

COMMUNITY IS COSTLY

Community asks of us:

Vulnerability
The laying down of prayer
Trust
Commitment to others
Accountability
Faithfulness
Giving and receiving of forgiveness
Openness

Acceptance of diversity
Kindness
Risking of ourselves

Silent reflection

O God, we are many times afraid of our calling to community.

Voice 1:
We would prefer to travel without responsibility.

Voice 2:
We would rather not risk being hurt.

Voice 3:
We find it more comfortable to have structures of power.

Voice 4:
We sometimes choose to stay with our guilt
and separate ourselves from your community.

**Forgive us, O God, and help us to remember that we are
your body.**

ASSURANCE OF PARDON

We are always the broken body but the word to us
is that in Jesus Christ we are made whole
and enough to do the task.

READINGS

CELEBRATION OF COMMUNITY

We are living stones in the holy city of God.
Let us take a stone and say what sort of stone we are
as we place it in the centre.

*The people name themselves and place a stone on the communion
table or in the centre of the group*

LITANY OF AFFIRMATION

We are the royal children of God:
Those who join the whole communion of saints,
honoured of God
respected by Christ
and befriended by the Holy Spirit.

We are the people whose tears fall
for the suffering of the world.
We truly care
about the world in which we live,
even as we feel our lack of power,
and our need for wisdom.

We are the people of hope and faith.
Together we will celebrate
the moments of new life.
Together we will work and play.
Together we will give thanks
for the gifts along the way.
Amen.

BLESSING

Go in peace.
We go as one people.
We go as the loved community of God.

And may God be at our beginning,
Christ be in our centre,
and the Spirit be there in our endings.
Amen.

THE GOLDEN ONES

A Eucharist for people who feel marginalized

You will need for this service

- *Small candles.*
- *Elements for a Eucharist.*
- *A golden cloth to be draped from the table.*

GREETING

The peace of Christ be with you.
And also with you.

OPENING SENTENCES

We are the golden children of God:
**Lying below the surface of life's earth
in hidden beauty and value.**

We wait to be discovered:
**As the Divine waits in everyone,
full of loving humanness.**

In us the Spirit dances and sings:
**Found in the melody of possible music
which hums and moves in all creation.
Thanks be to God!**

IT'S NOT EASY

It's not easy being who we are, O God.
We often wonder what you are doing,
not because we have problems about being who we are
but because others do.
They have so much power to take life from us,
create so much fear in us
that the claiming of our life
becomes an endless act of courage.

We are tired of hiding ourselves
and explaining ourselves
and limiting ourselves, O God.
We do not wish to deny ourselves any longer
because it destroys the wholeness to which we are called.
Free us to life, to love and justice, O God who made us.

ASSURANCE OF PARDON

In Christ, we share the road with the one who wept
over Jerusalem
and walked towards the oppressors there
with costly hope and trembling faith.
Amen.

READINGS

Silent reflection

AFFIRMATION OF FAITH

In response to the word, let us affirm our faith:

**In the God of all creation,
we have our life and being,
children of divine imagination
born from love,
for freedom and for truth and human being.**

**In the God in Christ,
we see the vision for our journeying,
walking unknown paths
through crucifixions and resurrections,
treading past our bleeding with passionate hearts
into small spaces where life is reborn.**

**In the Spirit of joy and dreams
we live on in the face of the struggle,
laughing and weeping in the centre of our pain,**

celebrating in the power of our solidarity
with all who stand for love and hope
and the victory of right.

WE NEED HELP

Let us light a candle for those we trust to be our
    support in this journey:

The people say the names and light candles

And God will be our help
in this time of struggle,
in the days and nights of our fearfulness
and need for courage.
We hope for energy and wisdom,
for resources of strength,
for companions when the way is lonely
and for a sense that we are indeed the children of good.

We pray for all who are rejected and patronized,
all who have suffered at the hands of the Church
when it betrays its God.
Give to them comfort and certainty
in their determination to live.
Give to us all these gifts, O God,
for we ask for them in faith.
Amen.

OFFERTORY

GREAT THANKSGIVING

Christ be with you!
And also with you.

Lift up your hearts!
We lift them up to God.

Let us give thanks to the Holy God.
It is right to give our thanks and praise.

Holy God, we praise and thank you
for all the creativity we find in ourselves,
for your respecting of the struggles of your creation,
even our struggles,
and for the ripples of your grace
which flow forth eternally in all that is.
We thank you for Jesus Christ,
who walked within all of our reality,
stood in the centre of our betrayals
and with all integrity
claimed the glory of life,
hard won, and coloured deep
with the blood of our pain.
God in the torn apart,
God in the wholeness,
God in the emptiness,
God in the fullnesses,
you are always God with us.

And so we praise you . . .

INSTITUTION

MEMORIAL PRAYER

As we break this bread
and share this wine:
we receive a God
who is at the centre of our brokenness
and the brokenness of the world,
and we drink a cup
which we all hold in common.

As we wait in faith
for the healing love of Christ:
we sing of a dream of reborn hope
and the power of love.

THE EUCHARIST CONTINUES . . .

THANKSGIVING AFTER COMMUNION

Let us pray:

**We thank you, gracious God,
that we are the guests at your table.
As we have been fed by your gifts of life,
so we will share with the world
all that you give to us in love.
Amen.**

COMMISSIONING AND BLESSING

Take up the task with hope and faith!
We believe that we are the children of God.

The world is always waiting for us to emerge:
so, go with courage into the costly path of Christ,
go with imagination into the creative life of God
and go with freedom into the life of the Spirit.
Amen.

Hard Times, Sad Times

O God who travels with us in the shadows,
you know who we are.
We long for life which is full and free.
We long to know the truth
and we want to leave behind us
all the things which hold us back.

LITURGY FOR HARD JOURNEYS

This service was originally prepared for someone dealing in a painful way with abuse in her early life. It can be used or adapted for others with painful experiences in their past.

It deliberately begins with a sense of a corporate journey, so that person resumes her/his place in the community and its journey.

For this service you will need

- *A beautiful candle to present to the person concerned.*
- *Oil for anointing for healing.*

GREETING

Life is a journey on many different roads
but God is always with us.

Sometimes we lift our faces to the sun
and God is with us.

But then there is the hard journey
through pathways of pain
and fears in dark places.
But God is with us.
Nothing can separate us
from the love of God in Christ Jesus.

WHO WE ARE ON THE JOURNEY

O God who travels with us in the shadows,
you know who we are.
We long for life which is full and free.
We long to know the truth

and we want to leave behind us
all the things which hold us back.

Silent reflection

We want to move forward in faith
but the way seems so dangerous
and we stand in helpless fear
before that which is hidden in our past
and in our future.

Silent reflection

Stand beside us, gentle Christ.
Walk before us, brave Jesus.
Call us on into life, Holy Spirit.
Amen.

WE ARE NOT ALONE

Hear the word to us in Jesus Christ:
I will never leave you nor forsake you,
even to the end of time.
I will walk with you
down the pathways of death
and lead you to eternal life.
Amen.
Amen.

READINGS

Suggested: Isaiah 43.1–5; 49.13–16a

LIGHTING OF THE CANDLE

The candle is the sign of the light, warmth and power of the
Holy Spirit.

The candle is lit and the person on the hard journey is asked to
come near to the candle

See the light for your journey
and believe that the Spirit always

moves ahead of you.
Stretch out your hands
and feel the warmth of the flame.
It is the warmth of the love of God for you
and our love for you.
That love will surround you wherever you go.
Take into yourself the power of the Holy Spirit
that you may be given courage
for the next step on the journey.

The person on the journey kneels and those present gather around
for the anointing and the laying on of hands

We are the body of Christ for you.
As our hands are upon you
so you are one with Jesus Christ
   who heals us
   comforts us
   protects us
and lifts us up to walk forward again.
As we anoint you with the sign of the cross,
   we claim the power
   of God the loving parent
   God in Jesus Christ
   and God the Holy Spirit for you.
Receive all these gifts
and claim the life that is before you.

PRAYERS OF INTERCESSION

Prayers for the particular person can be prepared and said by some
of the gathered friends and then the candle is given to the person

BLESSING

A blessing, such as the Aaronic blessing, can be sung or another
said as follows

Go in peace,
the peace which passes understanding.

And may the God who is your loving parent stand between you
    and all harm,
the God of loving-kindness look upon you with grace
and the Spirit visit you with healing and peace.
Amen.

DARE TO FEEL THE LONGINGS

For those who want to share in God's work but find it hard

You need for this service

* *A basket of flowers, enough for one for each of those gathered.*

OPENING SENTENCES

Sisters and brothers, will we take the risk
of seeing our world through the eyes of God?
With God's help, we will.

Will we hear and taste and smell the poor of the earth
and walk towards the Christ who is already there?
With God's help, we will.

Will we so believe in the grace of God that
we can dare to feel the longings of the people
mingled with our own frailty?
With God's help, we will.
We are not alone.

KNOWING WHO WE ARE

Let us look upon the world, the holy ground of God,
even as we remember who we are.

Silence

We are not heroic, O God.
We are your ordinary people.
Christ, have mercy.

Sung twice or said:

Lord have mercy.
Christ have mercy.
Lord have mercy.

ASSURANCE OF PARDON

Rise, take up your bed and walk.
The Christ is never defeated by our humanness.
Amen.
Thanks be to God!

READINGS

Silent reflection

GATHERING OF THOSE WE SEE

Let us gather in the people and the situations
which we see reflected with concern in the eyes of God.

*The people and situations are gathered in as the people
remember them*

Dear God, we hold these people and situations in our hearts
and gather them into the hollow of your loving hand.

NAMING OUR NEEDS

What do we need from God to hold us into the
rigour and passion and cost of this adventure?
What would help us take the risk of standing
in solidarity with God's children?

The people name their needs

Come, O Holy Spirit.
Come, O Holy Spirit.

*The basket of flowers from the table is passed around and each
person takes a flower*

OFFERING

What have we to offer to God
and the world which God loves?

The people make their offering – sharing their hopes about what each could do in a small way, and then making their money gifts

Receive these our gifts, O God.
**Take them and bring them into the blossoming
of your overflowing life.
Amen.**

BLESSING

God is a God who takes infinite risks
with people like us.
Go in faith and hope to be part of the
recreating of the world.
Amen.

A SERVICE OF HEALING

This service was prepared for an individual who needs healing or forgiveness. Those present are people who are there to be the community of faith around the person, in whatever way that is appropriate – they may be invited friends or family representatives from a congregation.

For this service, you need

- *Oil for anointing.*
- *A simple chalice-like cup – something like a wine-glass to be given to the one asking for healing.*

WITNESS

In Jesus Christ, we hear the Good News
that God is like a mother hen
who shelters her chickens
under her warm wings.
We believe that God is love.

In Jesus, we see a God
who wept for the people of the world,
and weeps for our wounding.

In Jesus, we see a God
who reaches out with healing hands,
who sees our pain and makes us whole.

CONFESSION

Let us join in our prayers of confession:

O God, you die for us and conquer death for us,
but we find it hard to believe in your love.

We see your creativity in all the earth,
but fear to ask for our own healing.
Forgive us and bring us to faith.

ASSURANCE OF PARDON

Hear the word to us in Christ:
If we have faith as small as a mustard seed,
God's power is released in us.
Our healing is a gracious gift.
Rise, take up your bed and walk.
Amen.
Amen!

READINGS

Suggested: Psalm 13; Luke 8.43–8

SERMON

PRAYERS OF INTERCESSION

O God, we cry to you in our anger
that people hurt each other.
Be with us and heal us, O God.

We feel the fear and pain
of an innocent and trusting child.
Be with us and heal us, O God.

We carry with us the things
that have been done to us
which hurt and destroy.
Be with us and heal us, O God.

They stand before us
and weigh us down.
They stop us living with joy and hope.
Be with us and heal us, O God.

Lift us up on the wings of your Spirit.
**Set us free with your peace
and your power.**

For you are stronger
than all the forces that stand against us.
Set us free,
heal our wounds,
O God who never leaves us
nor forsakes us.
Amen.

LAYING ON OF HANDS

If you wish to receive the laying on of hands and personal
prayer for healing, please come and kneel at the front.

The person seeking healing kneels and those present gather around

Minister:

We lay our hands upon you in the name of Jesus Christ,
healer and lover of the world.

Silent prayer

May the Lord of love,
who is more powerful
than all those who would harm us,
give you healing for all that is past
and peace for all that is to come.
May she surround you with comfort and warmth
and fill you with life that is stronger than death.
Amen.
Amen!

ANOINTING

Minister:

Lift your face to the light.
You are beautiful in the sight of God.
The mark of Christ is upon you;
walk free and open your heart to life,
for Christ walks with you
into a new day.
Amen.

The person is anointed

People:

Amen!

SHARING OF THE COMMON CUP

The cup is passed between the people with the words:

We share life with you.

After the cup is shared, the minister gives the cup to the person who seeks healing and says:

Take this cup as a sign
of our community with you.
Your tears are our tears;
your hope is our hope;
your prayer is our prayer;
you are not alone.

PEACE

The peace of God be with you all.
And also with you.

The people exchange the peace

BLESSING AND DISMISSAL

Go in peace
and may God the Mother keep you safe,
God the Father hold you firmly,
God in Christ take you by the hand,
and God the Spirit cover you
with her warm bright wings.
Amen.
Amen.

LIGHT A CANDLE

This is a Taizé-style service of healing for congregational use.

Introduction
When entering a healing service, the congregation needs a clear understanding of its own theology of healing so that it can proceed with confidence. For example: When we pray for healing, we pray with confidence and expect to receive a response from a loving God. We are not God. Therefore, although we ask for healing as though we are speaking to a loving parent, we cannot determine the answer. When we pray, we believe that we bring together all our love, healing and energy with the powerful healing love and energy of God. We wait with faith and expectancy for the gifts to be given.

For this service you will need

- *Numbers of candles arranged in a central spot, with tapers for lighting.*
- *The baptismal font, filled with water and in a central place.*

GREETING

Christ be with you!
And also with you.

Let us worship God.

APPROACH

O God, you brought forth light out of darkness
and out of nothing you created the universe.
**With awe and trembling hearts
we come into the mystery of your presence.**

O Christ, you lived among us;
you taught and healed us
and showed your great love
by embracing the bitter cross.

**With longing and hope
we come into the mystery of your presence.**

O Holy Spirit,
you come to us in the rushing wind and fire,
bringing strength and comforting and healing.
**With open hearts and minds
we come into the mystery of your presence.
We praise you, loving God.
Be in our midst today,
bringing light, love and strength.
Amen.**

GLORIA

Sung (Taizé)

CONFESSION

2 Samuel 12.1–14

There was a time when people believed
that God would kill a child for the sin of its father or mother
– and some people still believe that today.

Sung (Taizé):

Kyrie, Kyrie, eleison.

There was a time when they believed
that God sent war to punish one guilty person
by killing and maiming thousands.
Some still believe this.
Kyrie, Kyrie, eleison.

There was a time when people believed,
and there are some of us, sometimes still,
who believe God needs persuading to be merciful.
Kyrie, Kyrie, eleison.

There was a time when many of us on a bad day believed
that God sends famine and sickness and misfortune
to those who would rouse her anger
and sometimes we still believe that.
Kyrie, Kyrie, eleison.

There was a time not so long ago,
when we believed that healing was a sort of lottery:
some are lucky, some are not,
according to God's whim.
Kyrie, Kyrie, eleison.

There are times for all of us,
when God appears absent, asleep, indifferent, dead.
Kyrie, Kyrie, eleison.

Silence

CHANT

'By night we travel in darkness' *(Taizé)*

ASSURANCE OF PARDON

The faithfulness of God is greater than our doubt.
The innocence of Christ is stronger than our guilt.
The Spirit of love surrounds us here and now,
to make us whole.
Thanks be to God!

LIGHTING OF CANDLES

*People are invited to come forward and join the children to light a
candle, or wash their hands in the font*

CHANT

'Bless the Lord, my soul' *(Taizé)*

GOSPEL

SERMON

AFFIRMATION OF FAITH

Seated

Let us affirm our faith:

**We believe in God
whose breath brings the gift of life;
whose creativity makes newness out of nothing;
whose love sent us the Christ;
whose solidarity accompanies our deaths;
whose power frees us to the resurrection;
whose Spirit liberates us from powerlessness;
whose grace stands under all our being;
whose unity calls us to be the Church
and to live out the hope of the kingdom.**

THE LORD'S PRAYER

SILENT PRAYER

CHANT

'Come, O Holy Spirit' *(Taizé)*

*During the chant, people are invited to come to the centre of the
church to share in and receive the laying on of hands*

CHANT

'Come, O Holy Spirit' *(Taizé)*

PRAYER FOR HEALING

Spirit of God,
enter the life of this your loved child.
Come with your healing, your peace and your freedom.
We claim now your transforming power and love.

This may be repeated as often as necessary for all who wish to receive the laying on of hands

INTERCESSIONS

Prayer of St Francis *(sung)*

'Make me a channel of your peace' *or other suitable hymn*

You are invited to light a candle for particular people or situations and if you wish, share your prayer with the congregation

CHANT

Softly: 'O Christe, Domine Jesu' *(Taizé)*

OFFERING

Let us bring our offering before God.

PRAYER OF DEDICATION

Receive these our gifts, O God.
**We bring them to share with the world
your grace and love.**

BENEDICTION

Go forth into the world to take up your tasks.
And may God's presence enlighten your way,
Christ's love surround you,
and the Holy Spirit be your strength.
Amen.

CHANT

'My peace I leave you, my peace I give you' *(Taizé)*

As we sing the final chant you are invited to extinguish a candle and quietly leave the church

AN ANOINTING

For a group of people who feel wounded or betrayed

This service can be adapted for a service which focuses on personal healing.

For this service you need

- *A small glass bowl of salt water for 'tears'.*
- *A container of fragrant oil.*

GREETING

Christ be with you.
And also with you.

OPENING SENTENCES

Our God is a God who longs to be with us:
**Who reaches into our deepest places,
who weeps within our tears.**

Our God is a God who holds us in the womb-space
    of compassion:
**Labouring to bring us to birth in the new life of freedom,
tasting the blood of our pain.**

Our God is like a rock:
**Unmoved from love,
unshaken by the anger in our righteous protest
firm beneath our feet
in the eternal creating of our holy ground.**

THE GRIEVING JOURNEY

Let us recall the journey of grieving,
the place of safety and joy which has been left
and the loss along the way:

The grievings, losses and disappointments are named

Let us taste the tears in this journey we have had together:

The bowl of tears is shared and the pain honoured in silence

THE WORD

Readings

Silent reflection

AFFIRMATION OF FAITH

Let us affirm our faith:

**There is no death
from which you cannot rise in us, O God.
The power to fail
can never kill the gift of life,
unless we choose not to receive it from you.
Your Spirit is never defeated
by the woundings of life
however unjust, however painful.**

**Your grace in Christ
goes well beyond our understanding
and your love for us is never measured
by our love for ourselves.
Even as we walk a hard journey
we will claim together
this great hope.
Amen.**

PRAYERS OF INTERCESSION

Let us place in the hands of God,
all that disturbs us,
all our longings for those who we hold in loving concern:

The people share their prayers

O Lord, hear our prayer.

Sung (Taizé):
O Lord, hear our prayer, O Lord, hear our prayer
Repeat

ANOINTING

In the name of Christ,
who has walked every journey before you
and sees deeply into your heart in understanding,
we announce a new day.
Receive the grace of God
and the healing of the Holy Spirit,
in the name of Christ,
Amen.

*The people pass to each other a pot of fragrant oil and anoint each
other on the hand or forehead with the words:*
Receive the grace of God.

BLESSING

Go in peace.
And may the God of grace encircle your soul,
the God in Christ reach out to touch you
and the Spirit shine light on your path.
Amen.

A SIMPLE FUNERAL

I have often used this service during my ministry because I find that, for many people, ministry is more effective when the Church uses a simplicity of liturgical style, most especially if the people concerned have little or no connection with the Church. I always make it clear that I am a Christian minister but indicate that I believe it is both respectful and self-respecting when the Church does not pretend a relationship which is not there. Obviously there are many adaptations to be made according to the honest realities of the person concerned.

I owe the idea of moving to touch the casket and the addressing of the person who has died to the Maori people of Aeteoroa New Zealand. I have found that this diminishes the feeling of the lonely casket and also the 'untouchability' of death. Sometimes I have found it helpful to use this moment to tell the person who has died something which a member of the family wishes they had said to the person. For example, 'Mary feels she never really told you how much she loves you. She does love you deeply, John.' Obviously, it is not helpful to take this too far. It is not meant to become a sort of confessional!

OPENING

Friends,
we have come together
because we loved (*Name*)
as (*mother, brother, family, friend, etc.*).
Here we will mourn her/him leaving us,
honour her/his life and death,
reverently farewell her/his body
and comfort each other.

We have come believing that all human life is valuable,
that the truth and integrity and hopefulness
which resides in each life, lives on.
We come, believing that (*Name's*) life,
which we celebrate today

and for which we now experience great loss,
is joined in the eternal continuum of human endeavour
stretching into the past and into the future.

Her/his life was lived in its uniqueness with us
and has now passed into the ultimate community
of human existence.
The gifts and graces which she/he offered are never lost to us.
The creativity which she/he brought to us
in her/his life and relationships lies now within our own lives
and travels into the future with us.

If appropriate:
Our lives are more beautiful because we lived with her/him.

PRAYER
or silent reflection

O God, at this moment,
as we come face to face with death
and our own mortality,
we have many feelings
as well as grief,
and possibly fear for the future.
Please come close to us with your love,
travel with us into this serious moment
and open our hearts to each other.
We ask it in the name of Jesus Christ
who faced his own death and the death of a friend.
Amen.

THE LORD'S PRAYER
if appropriate

READINGS
Traditional and/or contemporary

REFLECTION

None of us knows the whole truth about what lies beyond death.
Christians believe that as we journey between life and death,
    we are safe in the hands of an infinitely gracious God.
We believe that death invites us into total awareness and to
    know with truth whether what we have valued in ourselves
    has eternal value.
The God who stands with us at that moment is the same God
    who was prepared to die in love for all humankind, a God
    who has entered every struggle of our life with us and
    who deeply understands the choices we have made.

TRIBUTE

The things we would like to remember about the person

The minister moves to the casket and placing a hand on it says:

(*Name*), all these things and more you have given to us.
We respect your journey through life,
with all of its realities.
We pray that you will travel safely
in this next part of your journey.
Our love goes with you.
Let us pray or reflect in silence on this life and what it has
    meant to us:

Silent prayer/reflection

Thanks be to God for the gifts we have received in this person.
Thanks be to God for a life lived with (*courage, honesty, grace,
    determination – as appropriate*).

If a burial:
We will now accompany you to your final resting place.

The casket is carried to the grave

FAREWELL

As we come to the moment of farewell,
part of our grief may be regret

for things done or left undone,
words said, or never said,
or moments that never happened.
This is the time to lay aside all those regrets
and to honour the spirit of (*Name*) herself/himself
who would never want them carried into our future.
Let us receive that gift of generosity from (*Name*)
and the forgiveness of God.

Silent reflection

To love someone is to risk the pain of parting.
Not to love is never to have lived.
The grief which we now experience is the honouring of our love.
Let us now in a quiet moment
make our farewell to (*Name*).

Silence

COMMITTAL

If a burial:

And now let us commit her/his body to the earth
which is welcoming to us at the time of our death.
Ashes to ashes, dust to dust.
In the cycle of life and death the earth is replenished
and life is eternally renewed.

If a cremation:

And now let us commit her/his body to the elements
which are gentle to us at the time of our death.
Ashes to ashes, dust to dust.
In the cycle of life and death the earth is replenished
and life is eternally renewed.

Go in peace, (*Name*).
Travel safely with our love
into the hands of God.
Amen.

BLESSING AND DISMISSAL

Even as we grieve this loss,
let us commit ourselves to the comfort of those who miss
    her/him most
especially (*Names*).
Let us surround them with our love
and pray for the comfort of God.

And now let us go into the world,
glad that we have loved,
free to weep for the one we have lost,
free to hold each other in our human frailty,
empowered to live life to the full
(*if appropriate*) as did (*Name*)
and to affirm the hope of human existence.
And may God be our company,
Christ Jesus walk before us
and the Spirit surround us with a cloud of grace.
Amen.

The Christian Year

Here, among our everyday places,
here, among our ordinary lives,
is the emerging of grace.
Watch, watch, for the signs of the Holy.
In this time,
in every time,
we hold our breath in awe
for the wonder of the Christ.

LITURGY FOR ADVENT

For this service you will need

• *An Advent wreath with Advent candles.*

CALL TO WORSHIP

Among us the Spirit of God conceives new life,
and we feel the life within us.

In our history the Christ makes gentle entry,
and we see the light before us.

Within our dreams the truth of our God is revealed;
we await the hope of the world.

LIGHTING OF THE ADVENT CANDLE

Mary of Nazareth,
flowing bravely
with all the possibilities
for life,
touching close the deep centres
of being,
and present to the Holy Spirit
of God,
creating and moving
and bursting through
membranes of pain and doubt,
through labour-filled passages
into the light
of the star-shine world
and the poor,
who kneel in hope
before the sign of God.

The candle is lit

**O God, give to us all the eyes and heart of Mary,
who saw the vision for the liberation of the world,
and with love and courage committed herself
to live out that hope.
Amen.**

CONFESSION

In silence,
let us reflect on moments in our own lives
and in the life of the Church
when we have experienced
the life-giving movement of the Holy Spirit
and have allowed it to die –

moments when we have had
a sense of grief about ourselves,
a sense of betraying our own possibilities.

Silent reflection

In weakness,
in smallness of hope,
in vulnerable faith,
we stand before you, O God.
**We come in penitence
and await your renewing Spirit.**

ASSURANCE OF PARDON

Where the Spirit of the Lord is,
there is liberty!
God is always faithful to us
and gives to us a new day.
Amen.
Amen!

READINGS
Old Testament
Epistle

GOSPEL

SERMON

AFFIRMATION OF FAITH

Let us stand and affirm our faith:

We believe in God
who lives and speaks in sunsets,
in love-wrapped gifts,
and fleeting butterflies;
in women weeping strongly
for stillborn dreams
and hopes they never conceived.
We believe in God,
indwelling wholly,
in suffering and celebration.

We believe in Christ,
honouring our humanness,
who took nourishment
from a woman's breasts;
who climbed trees,
skinned knees;
who laughed and cried,
loved and wept,
bled and died.
We believe in the Christ,
sanctifying life, and death.

We believe in the Spirit,
mystically joining us
to peoples everywhere;
who intercedes
with sighs and groans

too deep for words;
a shared consuming struggle
bending our will to God.
**We believe in the Holy Spirit
incorporating us
into Christ.**

We believe in the Church,
being and becoming,
chosen as God's presence in the world
despite its frailty,
its foolishness,
its failings.
**We believe in the Church,
seeking, however imperfectly,
to act justly,
love mercy,
and walk humbly with our God.**

PRAYERS OF INTERCESSION

Let us join together in our prayers of intercession.
Our loving Parent, God,
who can be Mother as well as Father,
grant us the ability
to be constantly aware
that we are always in your presence.
You are the Ground of our Being.

We thank you for your presence in the world
that in our pain and anguish,
dance and song,
you are there.
**You are the Ground of our Being.
Everything that is.**

We remember those
for whom life seems unbearable;
for those whose spirit

weighs them down near death.
May they find in you
a hope that will sustain them.
You are the Ground of our Being.
Everything that is –
is because of you.

We thank you for the gift
which enables us
to see and hear
to think, and feel, and smell –
the suffering, the poverty, and oppression
of our brothers and our sisters everywhere.
May your Spirit ever move us
to bring their lives before you
in love, in action, and in prayer.
You are the Ground of our Being.
Everything that is –
is because of you.
May we ever be
the expression of your presence
in the world.

And now, let those who will,
lift up their prayers for the Church
and the world . . .

The people make their prayers

O God, we have come before you
bringing our hopes and our fears.
We have come because you have called us
that we might experience afresh
your grace and peace.
Amen.
Amen.

OFFERING

Let us bring our offering before God.

DEDICATION

As Mary offered herself in her humanness,
so we offer our gifts to you, O God.
We bring them in faith.
We bring them in gratitude
for all that we have received.
Amen.

BLESSING AND DISMISSAL

Rejoice in Bethlehem,
two thousand years ago.
Rejoice in the life
that was conceived,
lived
and given for us.

Go in peace
to love and serve the world.
And may your waiting be in hope,
each day be lived in faith
and the love in Christmas be moving toward you.
Amen.

LITURGY FOR CHRISTMAS DAY

Needed for this service

- *An Advent wreath, with all candles lit except the Christ candle.*
- *Many other candles placed in clusters around the church for the children to light, and tapers to light them.*
- *Obviously many carols would be sung throughout this liturgy. Only one is mentioned because its placement is integral to the liturgy.*

OPENING

This is the moment.
This is the day of gladness,
the rebirthing of love!
Listen, listen, for the sounds of joy.

Here, among our everyday places,
here, among our ordinary lives,
is the emerging of grace.
Watch, watch, for the signs of the Holy.

In this time,
in every time,
we hold our breath in awe
for the wonder of the Christ.
For this is Christmas Day!

The Christ candle is lit

CONFESSION

O God, all around us we find situations
which take away our faith in the birth of love among us:

Silent reflection

If we have lost our sense of wonder and delight
and believe these things belong in children's stories alone:

Forgive us, God of sunrises and angel songs.

If we no longer expect surprises
and take the gifts of others and our own gifts for granted:
**Forgive us, God of babies in mangers in stables and
shepherds in fields.**

When love for the world seems an impossible dream
and we give power to cynicism
and a spirit of defeat:
Forgive us, God of the shining star of hope.

Silent reflection

ASSURANCE OF PARDON

Jesus Christ came into the world as it was,
in all its humanness.
So in every generation, love will come again.
Thanks be to God!

READINGS

SERMON

PRAYERS OF INTERCESSION

On this day, the day of gladness,
there are many people who feel, even more deeply,
the lack of love around them.
Our joy becomes almost an offence to them
as they struggle to survive.
God of love,
we remember before you those who are lonely,
who feel unloved and rejected,
who this day see their world as a place of depression
and despair.

Silent prayers

Prince of peace,
we remember before you those who have no peace,
those who live in places of war around the world,

The places are named

those whose personal lives have little peace within,
those whose homes are not places of peace today.

Silent prayers

God of justice,
we remember before you those who are oppressed,
those who find it hard to believe that you have come
to free the captives and to lift up the lowly ones.

The people share their prayers for situations of injustice

Dear God, the God in the vulnerable Child of Bethlehem,
we pray to you because we believe that you have come,
that you are a God above all Gods
who yet knows our life in Jesus Christ.
Amen.

THE LORD'S PRAYER

LITANY OF FAITH

Angel songs will rise above this grieving earth.
The melody of joy will sound in sweetness
beyond the weeping and despair.
Sing out the carols of this day.
Jesus Christ has come!

A carol is sung

The light of the stars of hope
will never be dimmed.
They will shine forth forever in visions of wisdom
into the dark night of the people.
Light the flames of warmth to welcome the one
who comes to end the coldness of the lonely journeys!

The children light candles all around the church

The child of love is abroad in all the earth,
liberating those who are bound,
standing with those who struggle for justice,
breathing a costly life into peace.
Lift up the hearts of the people!
Share the goodness of God.
Into every place of need,
Jesus Christ has come!

The offering is received

O God of love,
receive our gifts and with them
the thanksgiving in our hearts for this day.
We kneel before the wonder of your coming,
as did the people of old.
We will carry your love into the world.
Amen.

BLESSING AND DISMISSAL

Go in faith and joy.
And may the Prince of Peace dwell in every home,
the Child of gentleness be discovered in our midst
and this Holy Day lead to another and another.
Amen!

LITURGY FOR GOOD FRIDAY

This service was prepared by the Worship Committee of the Pitt Street Uniting Church in the centre of Sydney and is reproduced here with permission. It has been used by many congregations around the world and is well worth the effort in preparation. Pitt Street had its largest congregations on Good Friday because it understood the connections between the suffering of Christ and the lives of wounded, failing and fragile people.

The sermon which was originally preached with this liturgy focused on the theme that as we bring the hard things in our life to the cross and leave them there in faith, they are absorbed into the Body of Christ for transformation and healing. Many people bear witness to being healed during this liturgy.

For this service you need

- *A cross upright in a stand, initially at the front of the church but which can be lifted out of the stand to be placed on the floor in a central space during the service. This space needs to be large enough for people to move around it when the cross is lying on the floor.*
- *A bowl of rose petals or other, preferably fragrant, flowers or herbs in a basket on a table near the upright cross.*
- *A white sheet folded on a front seat (the shroud).*
- *A basket of good-sized stones near the centre of the church.*

INTRODUCTION

In this service for Good Friday, we will use periods of silence and Taizé chants which are repeated, often many times, so we have time for reflection and meditation. Please feel free to move about, in the music, finding your own level of harmony. Move about the worship space, finding the place that feels right for you. Sometimes the people are invited to move and take part in a ritual. Please feel free to join in or to stay quietly in your seat.

GREETING

We gather again on this Good Friday
at the foot of the cross
which calls us on,
  not in shame,
  not in fear
but more deeply into the costly journey
  towards life.
There is wounding,
there is weeping.
In Jesus Christ,
God is not separated from that.

CALL TO WORSHIP

In the shadow of our suffering
is the suffering of Jesus.

In the shadow of our weakness
is the vulnerability of the Christ.

In the shadow of our pain
is the God who cried out.

We are never rejected,
we are never left alone.

CHANT

'By night we travel in darkness' *(Taizé)*

MOVING CLOSER TOWARDS OURSELVES

First reading: Luke 23.1–32

God in Christ,
you travel with us in faith
  towards the hard places in our souls.

You know the agony of pain, guilt and hurt
    deep within us.
You know our own frightened faces,
    often hidden from ourselves.
You know the violence sometimes hurled in anger
because we feel powerless to take
    the smallest step to freedom.
You know the grief sometimes lying there
embalmed and perfumed
by our resolve
to remain victims forever.

There are stumbling blocks within ourselves
in our travelling, O God.
We take these stones and lay them
at the foot of the cross
which is able to bear the weight
and the wounding for us.

The people take stones to represent their hard things, bring them forward and leave them at the foot of the cross

CHANT

'By night we travel in darkness' *(Taizé)*

Silence

We leave these hard things here on our way through to life.

Silence

Second reading: Luke 23.33–54

The reader reads Luke 23.33–48, then says:
All his friends stood at a distance, and they saw all this happen.

Four people lift the cross from its stand, and hold it like a coffin

Reader:

When it was evening, there came a rich man of Arimathea, called Joseph, who had become a disciple of Jesus. He went to Pilate and asked for the body of Jesus. It was handed over to him.

Two people lay out the shroud in the middle of the church

Reader:

Joseph took the body, wrapped it in a clean shroud, and put it in his own new tomb which he had hewn out of the rock.

CHANT

'O Christe Domine Jesu' (*Taizé*)
This chant continues while the bearers carry the cross down into the church and place it on the shroud

SERMON

Short silence

Reader:

Near the cross of Jesus stood his mother and his mother's sister, and Mary the wife of Clopas, and Mary of Magdala. Many women were there watching from a distance. Among them were the mother of Zebedee's sons, and Joanna, and Mary the mother of James and Joseph.

These women, who had travelled with Jesus from Galilee and looked after him, were following behind.

Mary watched the death of her innocent child and held him in her arms.

A woman takes rose petals from the bowl, and walks down to let them fall on the cross

We remember the death of our innocent selves.
We remember the death of innocent, fragile things in the world
around us.

CHANT

'O Christe Domine Jesu' *(Taizé)*

People take rose petals to the cross and touch it

It is time to leave this place.
Jesus said 'Father, into your hands
I commend my spirit.'

CHANT

'In our darkness' *(Taizé)*

AFFIRMATION OF FAITH

As we also commend ourselves into the hands of God, let us say
what we believe.

**We believe in God.
When there was nothing but an ocean of tears,
God sighed over the waters
and dreamed a small dream:
light in the darkness,
a small planet in space.**

**We believe in Jesus Christ.
When hate and fear were raging,
when love was beaten down,
when hope was nailed and left to die,
Christ entered into our deep secret places
and went down into our death to find us.**

**We believe in the Holy Spirit
who weeps with us in our despair,
who breathes on prison doors,**

never admitting it's hopeless,
always expecting the bars to bend and sway
and break forth into blossom.

Reader:
They took note of the tomb and of the position of the body.
Then they returned and prepared spices and ointments.
And on the Sabbath day they rested.

SENDING OUT

I send you out into the world
in the power of the spirit of Christ
to walk through darkness and uncertainty
towards the joy of Easter Day.
Go in peace.

CHANT

'My peace I leave you' *(Taizé)*

The people walk out quietly towards Easter Day

On Easter Day those preparing for the Easter Service at Pitt Street
came and lifted up the cross from the floor. They found a cross-shaped
empty space outlined by rose petals.

LITURGY FOR EASTER

For this service you need

- *Baskets of wheat seeds at the door from which people take a seed as they enter the church.*
- *An empty basket, placed on the communion table.*
- *A larger basket containing enough small bread rolls for all the people, at the foot of the communion table.*

GREETING

Christ be with you!
And also with you.

CELEBRATE THE SEEDS OF LIFE

Celebrate the seeds of life which lie within us.
Let us carry them on the way of the cross
and safely into risen life in Christ.

For God is with us,
around us and within us.
Life and love are stronger than death.
Thanks be to God!

ENTRY INTO DEATH

'Except a grain of wheat falls into the ground and dies,
it remains alone. But if it dies, it bears much fruit.'
The passion of Christ, the journey into Good Friday,
is an invitation to take the seed of life which is ours and
allow it to enter the darkness of its inner life
and the earthy darkness of the world around it.
Here we may safely face our pain and weakness, our failure
and griefs, our woundedness and our woundings.

Here, as we entrust that fragile seed to Jesus Christ,
we will be held by One who can receive all our reality

with understanding, grace and costly love.
Let us look at the wheat seed in our hands and, in the quiet,
dare to know who we are before God.

Silent reflection

Guard us on this journey, O Christ.
Keep us safe as we follow you in faith.

ASSURANCE OF PARDON

Nothing in heaven or on earth
can separate us from the love of God in Christ Jesus.
God forgives us, heals us and brings us to life.
Amen.

Sung: 'Bless the Lord my soul and bless God's holy name'
(Taizé) – repeat twice

READINGS

Silent reflection

SERMON

AFFIRMATION OF FAITH

In response to the word, let us stand and affirm our faith:

**We believe in God,
who when there was nothing
planted the seeds of life in all creation,
green in the desert,
blossoms in the trees
and breath in the clay of human life.**

**We believe in Jesus Christ,
eternal seed of life,
who entered the deaths of our existence,**

trod deeply into our earthiness,
took into his body all our painfulness,
and lifted it into the victory of love.

We believe in the Holy Spirit
who waters our grief with tears,
nourishes in us the buds of life,
and tenderly cherishes our growings
until they break forth
into the fruits of hope and faith.

INTERCESSION

As we look at ourselves, the Church and the world,
let us see the signs of the seeds of new life, however small.
If you wish, place the seeds from your hands in the basket on
    Christ's table,
where seeds are turned into bread,
and name the sign you see or the hope you have,
or name those hopes in the silence of your hearts before God:

The people place the seeds

O God, we are never without your hope of newness.
**We pray that you will take these fragile signs,
seeds of our longing,
and bring them to abundant life.
Amen.**

SETTING OF THE TABLE

This table stands among us,
Christ's table and our table.
**We gather around it
in our common humanness,
one people in our frailty,
none more worthy than the other,
all made worthy in the resurrection of Christ.**
The seeds of our life are joined on the table
with the life of Christ.

**With joy we bring the gifts of bread and wine,
in faith we name this our Holy table
as it carries the Body of Christ.**

THE EUCHARIST CONTINUES . . .

DISMISSAL AND BLESSING

As you brought with you the seed in your hand,
so believe that it always lies within you.
As you have received the life of Christ,
so take these small loaves
as the sign of the work of the Spirit in your midst
bringing forth the fruits of grace.

The loaves are passed around

Go in peace,
for Christ is risen!
**Christ is risen indeed!
We will go in joyful faith
And the Christ will go with us.
Amen.**

LITURGY FOR PENTECOST

The focus for this Pentecost service is the Spirit who is abroad in all the earth and in all its peoples. Some of its writing came from the Worship Committee of the Pitt Street Uniting Church in Sydney and is used with its permission.

Needed for this service

- *If possible, a red candle shaped like a flame with five wicks.*
- *If this is not available, four smaller red candles clustered around a larger red candle.*

OPENING SENTENCES

Let us worship God.
It is time!
Spirit, move in the belly of God.
Come, warm into the rock of our beginnings,
alive with original blessings.

Spirit, run in the streets of the city.
Flow to the deep brown roots of our belonging.

Spirit, invade the air.
Stretch widely with whispering wings,
and cover us with your healing.

Spirit, soar in the high towers and shop-fronts.
Carry the seed,
call the song
of the dance in the heart of God.
Wake us to hope and freedom.

CONFESSION

Let us join in our prayers of confession.
Spirit of joy, with us always,
through you, Christ lives in us, and we in Christ.

Forgive us when we forget you
and when we fail to live in your joy.

Sung: (Taizé)
Kyrie

Spirit of love, with us always.
You bind us in love to yourself
and to those around us.
Forgive us when we hurt those we love
and when we turn away
from the love of our friends.
Kyrie

Spirit of the Body of Christ, with us always,
uniting us in the Church
with your life-giving grace and hope.
Forgive us in our fragmenting of your Church
and our failure to carry your love into the world.
Kyrie

Spirit in our world, with us always,
comforting us, and drawing us
into closer relationship with each other.
Forgive us our wars and our hatreds,
forgive our failure to recognize you,
who lives in us all.
**The Spirit is with us
reconciling us to God.**

LIGHTING OF THE PENTECOST CANDLE

Reader 1:
The Spirit of faithfulness
is the gift of the earth.

A wick is lit

Reader 2:
The Spirit of imagination and variety
comes to us from many countries.

A wick is lit

Reader 3:
The Spirit of hope breathes
in the poor and homeless
in this city.

A wick is lit

Reader 4:
The Spirit of freedom
was announced by those who went before us
and we proclaim it again today.

A wick is lit

Leader:
The Spirit of love is Christ's gift to the Church
in every age.

The centre flame is lit

We see the flame of the Spirit of God.

*Candles are brought forward by representatives of various ethnic
backgrounds or countries*

Each representative:
The Spirit is alive in (*names country*).

We see the flame of the Spirit.

Leader:
The Spirit is
    dancing
    moving
    struggling
    rising
and calling to the ends of the earth.
We are forgiven and freed to new things.
**We have seen the flame of the Spirit
in our midst.
Thanks be to God!**

GLORIA

READINGS

SERMON

AFFIRMATION OF FAITH

Let us stand and affirm our faith.

**We believe
in God the creator
who gives birth to all that is
   with labour and sighing
and looks to the world with joy and love.**

**We believe
in Christ the reconciler,
who is earthed in our life
and enfleshed in its patterns of dying and rising,
who gives honour to our reality
and grace to our way.**

**We believe
in God the free Spirit,
who weeps with our grievings
in the depths of our darkness
and dances among us high on life's mountains –
the Spirit who finds us with newness and hope.**

**We believe
in the community of faith,
which is born of our humanness,
is nurtured in sharing
and grows whole in our struggling
and celebration
as one people of God.**

INTERCESSION

Let us join in prayer
for the work of the Spirit around the world.

The people bring their prayers for different countries

After each prayer the response:
Gracious God, hear us.

Spirit of justice,
Spirit of peace,
Spirit of Christ,
our comforter, advocate and guide,
we pray for your Church:
**May we ever reflect your life
and your love.
May we ever give power to
your light and the passionate
energy of your renewing spirit.
Amen.**

OFFERING

Let us bring our offerings to God.

The offering is received

SETTING OF THE TABLE

This table stands among us –
Christ's table
and our table.
**We gather around it
as did the first disciples,
humble people, who love Jesus,
hopeful people in the power of the Spirit.**

Little children stand under this Holy table,
old people hold on to it.
Symbols of our life are placed upon it.
With joy we dress it in colour and light.
**With joy we bring our gifts.
In faith we name it
our Holy table
as it carries the Body of Christ.**

The bread, the wine and the offerings of the people are placed on the table

GREAT THANKSGIVING

Christ be with you!
And also with you.

Lift up your hearts!
We lift them to our God.

Let us give thanks to the Holy God.
It is right to give our thanks and praise.

Creator God,
thank you
for the moving of the rock,
the dancing of life,
the running of the water,
the rising of the trees
and the birth of humankind.
Thank you
for the coming of Jesus Christ our Saviour;
for his life of joyful loving,
his dying
and his rising splendid.

Thank you
for the gift of the Spirit,
the flame of truth,
the wind of freedom,
the song of hope in every age.
With those who have gone before us
and those who will come after us,
we worship you
in songs of never-ending praise:

Holy, Holy, Holy . . .

INSTITUTION

THE EUCHARIST CONTINUES . . .

BLESSING
Go in peace.
And may God be in your creating,
Christ be found in your midst,
and the Spirit lead you to life.
Amen.
Amen!

Endings – and New Beginnings

Just when we think nothing new could be found in us,
all things known, all things gone as far as they can go:
You are born again within us,
God of new beginnings.

and

Even as we seem to be dying
in weakness,
in fear,
overwhelmed by all the forces against us,
there are moments when we know
that we will never be determined
by any of that.

BEING BORN AGAIN

A service to celebrate a new time in the life of people

For this service, you will need

- *Oil for anointing.*

OPENING SENTENCES

Just when we think nothing new could be found in us,
all things known, all things gone as far as they can go:
You are born again within us,
God of new beginnings.

Just as we think nothing can ever change,
all things established, embedded in old powers:
The transforming flow of your life is there among us,
God of new ways of being.

Just when the deathly cycles drag us down into nothingness,
all things despairing, all things destroying:
You rise in vivid life beyond our weak survivals,
God of new victories over death.
Thanks be to God.

WE WERE NOT EXPECTING A MIRACLE

Most of us were not expecting a miracle, O God.
Some of us were expecting a miracle,
but not for us.

Silent reflection

Many things hold us back from new possibilities:

the people share the things that hold them back

or:
fear of what it would mean to change,
the power of our past relationships in life,
hard experiences in our lives,
things which we have done or not done,
and discouragement
because we often cannot see too many signs of your reign
in us and in the world.

Silent reflection

We would like to expect miracles, O God.
Please give us faith,
and help us in our unbelief.

ASSURANCE OF PARDON

The word to us in Christ is that
if we have faith as much as a mustard seed,
that will be enough
for the transforming of us and the world.
Thanks be to God!

READING

Suggested: John 3.1–16

TESTIMONY

The person or people share experiences of being born again

Music or dance of celebration

*Those involved are encircled by the community of faith and anointed
as the royal children of God:*

Lift your faces to God and those who love you.

You are born again in the power of the Spirit.
Thanks be to God!

AFFIRMATION OF FAITH

In response to the word, let us celebrate our faith:

We celebrate the miracles of grace which change us,
born from the womb of God
and from the deeply respected struggles
of our bodies, minds, hearts and souls,
surrounded by costliness yet free for us
in the journey towards abundant life.

We celebrate
the moments when we are turned around
and look on ourselves and the world
as though we make new entry
and a different start
with living water for our thirst
and life-giving bread for our hunger.

We celebrate
the wonder of a creation
in which nothing is limited
to our horizons of sight
or boundaries of energy, courage or hope,
but which leaps forth
in amazing surprises of good
and endless transformations
towards its true fullness
in the imagination of God.

INTERCESSION

Hold this new birth in us, O God.
Keep it safe for growing.

Sustain this new faith in us, O God.
Keep it strong for hoping.

Direct this new power in us, O God.
Keep it only for good.

Cherish this new freedom in us, O God.
**Keep it true for the transformation of the world,
in your name.
Amen.**

BLESSING

Go in joy,
to sing with the whole creation
of the glory of God.
And God the Creator be the source of our life,
God in Christ rise in our midst
and the Spirit be wise in our ways.
Amen.

AND THE DANCE GOES ON

For this service, you will need

- *A small bird – if possible, one of the ones often found in souvenir shops which have feathers and are made of polystyrene and which feel warm in your hand.*

OPENING SENTENCES

We wondered whether we would have the energy:
or the heart for the on-going.

We felt the world, with all its desperation:
and relentless deathly cycles.

But, sometimes, for a moment,
it all becomes framed in light beyond our seeing.
In ourselves,
we feel the movement of possible music:
And in the imagination of God,
the birthings of Christ,
the dance goes on.

CONFESSION

Many things paralyse us, O God.
There is despair and fear,
endless struggle for enough resources,
confusion and too many discussions
because we would rather stand still
than make a mistake.

We often spend our energy struggling over small things
while the world groans in pain
and the cries of the people are more than we can bear.

We carry a heavy burden of guilt
while you are waiting to forgive us and free us

to lightness of heart and soul.
The way seems hard and we are often weary, O God.

Silent reflection and prayer

We come to you in humble faith.

ASSURANCE OF PARDON

Holding the small bird and showing it to the people

As God holds this small bird, in all its vulnerability,
so God holds each one of us and the world in loving care.
Rest in the hand of God for healing
and soon there will be freedom to fly.
Thanks be to God!

READINGS

REFLECTION

AFFIRMATION OF FAITH

Let us affirm our faith:

In God,
our deaths are not the final word,
our moments of crisis
are part of eternal possibility,
and our weakness
is taken up into the courage of God.

In Christ,
our humanness is touched with divine life,
our tears are mingled
with the longing love of Jesus,
and our solidarity with those who suffer
is joined by the Godly presence.

**In the Spirit,
there are no boundaries on the dream,
no endings to hope,
and a world beyond our seeing.
We will never live
beyond the cherishing of God.**

PRAYERS OF INTERCESSION

Let us share our hope in naming the parts of our life here,
and in the life of the world
which still waits for the cherishing of God:

*The people pass the small bird from one to the other and share their
prayers*

Peace is not with us yet,
racism and prejudice are not yet at an end,
people still live in poverty and injustice,
loneliness and despair is not yet gone:
**But for us,
the dance of the transforming Spirit goes on
and we announce a new community.
We claim it before it comes,
and we will join the dance of the Spirit of God.
Amen.**

BLESSING

Let us go in faith
to ponder in our hearts
the mystery of this moment.
And may life be born within you,
Christ Jesus be seen among you
and the Spirit move before us with joy.
Amen.

IN THE END – THERE IS A PASSION

OPENING SENTENCES

In the end – there is a passion:
deep in the heart of God.

It will not let us go:
**even if it travels with us
past the moments of death.**

It rises again and again
in the eternity of love:
a mystery, a wonder, God undefeated.

IT'S OFTEN HARD TO BELIEVE

It's hard to live with passion, God.
You lived that way,
always honest with yourself and other people,
even your friends;
always determined to take the risk
of living really free,
challenging powerful people,
actually caring about things
and they killed you.

Silent reflection

We never come close
to living as passionately as that, God,
but still it feels dangerous some of the time.
What if we make choices about our life
which seem to be the best we can do
and then we see them for what they are, and were,
and can't live with ourselves?
They were passionate decisions, God,
born of our blood, sweat and tears,
and we mostly thought you were in them
at least a little.

Silent reflection

Mostly we are just longing to be loved
and so we make our choices towards that.
It's hard for us to do otherwise.
You know that, God.
Some of it's about
wanting to keep what we have,
in power and in things
and maybe add a little more.

Silent reflection

You understand all that, God, who is Jesus.
You have felt all that we feel,
longed for all that we long for.
That's why, some of the time,
we manage to believe that you will forgive us.
Let us ask for the forgiveness of this God.
Forgive us and love us,
make sense of our struggles, O God of grace.

ASSURANCE OF PARDON

The assurance in Christ
is that this God loves us with such a passion
that God travels with us into death
and defeats that death forever.
Amen.
Thanks be to God!

READINGS

SERMON

or silent reflection

AFFIRMATION OF FAITH

Let us respond to the word:

Even as we seem to be dying
in weakness,
in fear,
overwhelmed by all the forces against us,
there are moments when we know
that we will never be determined
by any of that.

There is a God
who says to us
weep strongly,
be strongly afraid,
care strongly,
choose life strongly in faith
and I will live strongly
in all of that.

There is a God
who moves from hill to mountain top,
who stands high in the depths of the pit,
who gasps free of the waters of drowning
and plants the cross-shaped tree
on the very shaking ground on which we stand
as though our trembling earth is like a rock.

There is a God
who steps free
of the binding chains around our souls
and calls us in a voice
which always knows our name,
who always feels our pain,
who lifts our feet
as though our life
stands cupped in a saving hand
and cherished forever in a life-filled place.

CALL US ON

Call us on to the adventure
of your passionate life, O God.
**Carry us past the boundaries,
the near horizons of our small dreams.**

Paint our world in vivid colours
so that we see
a whole new vision of your possibilities.
**Hold the cup of living water to our lips
and breathe into our souls
the life of your Spirit.**

Pour over us the oil of your anointing
that we may stand tall
as the royal children of your birthing.
**Fill us with a fire
which burns from a flame of truth,
refining our beings
so that we dare to take in our hands
your cross of courage, justice, hope and love
and plant it abroad in all the earth.
We ask this in the name of the One
who walks this way before us
to the end of time.
Amen.**

BLESSING

Go forth in the miracle of the grace of God.
And may you be touched
by the fire of the Spirit,
the gentleness of the Christ
and the wisdom of your Maker.
Amen.

BEGINNING A NEW JOURNEY TOGETHER

OPENING SENTENCES

The hand of God encircles us:
God of our beginnings holding us firm.

The feet of Christ walk before us:
God of our journeying showing us the way.

The wings of the Spirit lift us up:
God who is our company, our energy, our joy.

FACING THE UNKNOWN

We may bring some vulnerable things to a new journey:
fear of the unknown,
a sense of inadequacy,
loneliness in a new group,
anxieties about coping with what lies ahead,
perhaps tiredness or unreadiness.

Let us, in faith and trust, share those things with each other
and be joined in our humanness:

The people name the more vulnerable things they bring to the journey

Jesus, remember us,
as we take up the grave responsibility of being the Church.

Sung three times: 'Jesus remember us, when you come into your
kingdom' *(Taizé)*

ASSURANCE OF PARDON

Hear the word in Christ to us:
Nothing in all creation can separate us from the love of God.
Rise up and walk in faith.
Amen.

READINGS

SERMON
Or silent reflection

AFFIRMATION OF FAITH
Let us respond to the word by affirming our faith:

**We believe in God
who created us from nothing
and goes on bringing to birth
new things beyond our imagining.**

**We believe in Jesus Christ
who entered our unknown journey
and experienced all our living,
who walked in our earthiness
and can still be discovered
in our midst.**

**We believe in the Holy Spirit
who calls us on to truth
in light beyond our seeing,
who stirs within our being
like a melody of possible music,
who dances on before us
in the freedom of passionate life.**

SHARING OUR HOPES BEFORE GOD
As we begin this journey together,
let us share our hopes and light a small candle
as a sign that the light of Christ travels with us in
these hopes:

*Each person names a hope or expectation for their journey and
lights a candle*

Now let us remember the hopes of the world and the
communities we have left behind:

The people share their prayers for others

O God, we place this our life in your hands.
Take all that we bring,
our gifts and talents,
our longings and our faith
and add your power for life,
for we ask it in the name of Jesus Christ.
Amen.

COMMITMENT TO EACH OTHER

As we are able, let us make our commitment
to walk together on this journey:

We will walk this way together,
with Jesus Christ in our midst.
Our hands are open to receive,
our hearts are open to give,
our minds long to learn
and our souls reach out to each other.
This time is eternal time for us
and God will be our blessing.
Amen.

DISMISSAL

Go into this moment in faith
and may the Holy God prepare a holy ground for you,
Christ Jesus take your hand on the way
and the Spirit surround you with grace.
Amen.

Index of Themes

Agape meal 23

Celebration 91, 115, 119, 122
Church, the 8
Cities 3, 105
Commitment 22, 49, 61, 69, 115,
    122, 125, 126, 128
Community 24, 25, 48, 51, 63, 64,
    126
Creation, the 32, 105

Eucharistic 8, 44, 51, 103, 109

Family/relationships 28
Fear/courage 59, 117, 120, 122,
    126
Freedom/playing 36

Gathering 24, 25, 48, 51, 63, 64,
    126

Grieving 20, 75, 78, 95
Group life 23, 25, 48, 51, 63, 64,
    126

Healing 61, 66, 70, 96
Holy Spirit 14, 122
Hope 20, 45, 51, 99, 101, 115, 119,
    122, 126
Humanness 25, 29, 30, 36, 96,
    121, 122, 126

Justice 19, 44, 45, 51, 63, 75, 126

Laying on of hands 68
Love 44, 66, 99, 121, 122

Mission 40, 63, 115, 119, 122,
    126

Unity 10

Index of Resources
for Worship

Affirmation of faith 5, 9, 21, 25,
30, 33, 37, 42, 45, 49, 52, 73, 76,
87, 99, 102, 108, 117, 120, 124,
127
Anointing 61, 68, 75, 77, 125
Assurance of pardon 3, 9, 14, 24,
28, 32, 37, 41, 44, 49, 52, 64, 67,
72, 92, 102, 116, 120, 123, 126

Blessing and dismissal 7, 12, 22,
26, 31, 35, 38, 43, 47, 50, 55, 61,
65, 69, 74, 77, 90, 94, 100, 104,
111, 118, 121, 125, 128

Call to worship/opening
sentences 3, 8, 13, 19, 23, 28,
32, 36, 40, 44, 48, 51, 63, 66, 70,
75, 85, 91, 96, 101, 105, 115,
119, 122, 126

Final thanksgiving 47, 55

Great thanksgiving 46, 53, 110
Greeting 28, 32, 59, 96

Litanies 15, 33, 93, 106

Offering/dedication of offering 7,
46, 64, 74, 90, 109

Prayers of Confession 3, 8, 13, 28,
32, 37, 40, 44, 51, 59, 63, 66, 71,
86, 91, 96, 101, 105, 115, 119,
122, 126
Prayers of Intercession 4, 10, 14,
31, 34, 38, 42, 45, 53, 64, 67, 73,
76, 88, 92, 104, 108, 121, 127

Readings 60, 97

The Society for Promoting Christian Knowledge (SPCK) was founded in 1698. It has as its purpose three main tasks:

- **Communicating the Christian faith in its rich diversity**
- **Helping people to understand the Christian faith and to develop their personal faith**
- **Equipping Christians for mission and ministry**

SPCK Worldwide serves the Church through Christian literature and communication projects in over 100 countries. Special schemes also provide books for those training for ministry in many parts of the developing world. SPCK Worldwide's ministry involves Churches of many traditions. This worldwide service depends upon the generosity of others and all gifts are spent wholly on ministry programmes, without deductions.

SPCK Bookshops support the life of the Christian community by making available a full range of Christian literature and other resources, and by providing support to bookstalls and book agents throughout the UK. SPCK Bookshops' mail order department meets the needs of overseas customers and those unable to have access to local bookshops.

SPCK Publishing produces Christian books and resources, covering a wide range of inspirational, pastoral, practical and academic subjects. Authors are drawn from many different Christian traditions, and publications aim to meet the needs of a wide variety of readers in the UK and throughout the world.

The Society does not necessarily endorse the individual views contained in its publications, but hopes they stimulate readers to think about and further develop their Christian faith.

For further information about the Society, please write to:
SPCK, Holy Trinity Church, Marylebone Road,
London NW1 4DU, United Kingdom.